Don't hang that breaking ball: How to not crush your job search, career or presentation

By Todd Hicks

Copyright in December 2016, revised in January 2020

About the book

There are only so many chances you get while seeking a job and any mistake, especially a significant one, can hurt your ability to find a steady job or even a temp job for many years - you may even feel as though you surrendered a mammoth homerun on a mistake pitch. Having experienced this, I wrote this book based on my personal experience.

I have made many job search mistakes and taken a public speaking course. Before landing a full-time, temp-to-hire job as a warehouse picker-packer eight months ago, I hadn't worked on a steady basis since leaving my job as a market research telephone interviewer in April 2000.

By reading this book, you will learn how to not blow your chances of getting hired plus you will learn how to keep your job and advance in your career. Also, you will learn other steps you have to take in order to land a position plus you will learn how to write a cover letter and a resume.

Speech management tips plus sales interaction tips and instruction on how to last on the job as a substitute teacher are also provided. As you exhibit the best possible interview, sales or speech presentation, you will win over the recruiter, your prospects or your audience more easily.

Introduction

Are you frustrated from having too much trouble landing a position? Being in your shoes for all these years, I understand what you are going through and want to help you overcome this before it's too late. The job market is cruel and unlike some people in the corporate world, I actually care about you.

Some recruiters who interview you may send you a letter thanking you for your time but not tell you what you did wrong (assuming you did) and some bosses will never warn you or tell you what you are doing wrong. Due to not wanting you to go down my path, I have written this book to give you the informational tools you must have in order to avoid blowing too many position appointments and going too long without having a steady job.

In addition to having many years of part-time work experience accumulated over time, I have had plenty of job interviews that did not go my way due to not being fully prepared or doing something dumb. Also, I've been let go from or reprimanded at a few of my jobs due to not being pleasant enough.

My poor career experience is my own doing to a vast extent. I have made mistakes on the job or in front of hiring managers I wish I could go back in time to do over. Akin to hanging a pitch that the batter drives for a 500-foot homerun and the World Series championship, any error you make in an interview or on the job can doom you and leave you with regret for a long time, especially if the employment market is mediocre at best like it is now and you are marginalized like me.

Although it is unfortunate I have made these mistakes, I have learned from them and will discuss them so that you do not go down this path - I'm nervous about my future. Because I have the desire to help a lot of other people not hurt their job searches so much that they spend so many years paying for it by never having a steady job in that stretch like I have, I created this book. As I am dedicated to helping you succeed, my purpose is to help you get the work you want and stay employed.

Until May 21, 2019, I had neither had a steady job nor had much of a chance to work as a temp for a long time. You must follow the steps below in order to avoid my predicament.

How to find and keep a job – section one

Dress the best you can on your way to any interview. No matter what place you are going to, the attire you wear can make or break you. One weekday in the summer of 1994, I made a telephone call to the Mexican-style fast-food restaurant I filled out a job application at.

As I spoke to one of their managers, he agreed to have me come in while letting me know that he could not promise me anything. Having an hour or slightly less to be there, I had no time to prepare. While that is not important, the method I used to get there was.

After my mom dropped me off about half-way on her way to work, I spent a while walking the rest of the way to the fast-food restaurant mentioned above in hot weather wearing a Polo shirt and shorts. Soon after I arrived, I had a brief interview – at the end of it, the manager told me to call to check up at the beginning of the following week.

When I called, he told me, "I decided not to. Okay, Todd?"

Although he gave no indication for declining to hire me and gave no indication that my lack of experience was a key factor, I know that I did not give myself more of a fighting chance by walking there in the summer and not wearing a suit, tie and dress shoes. By the way, do not neglect to ever ask why you are not being hired by a firm that interviewed you.

Neglecting to not do research prior to an appointment because of the work you seek can doom your job search for a long time. I hurt my chances of landing a teacher assistant position in 2001 or 2002. When one of the two recruiters asked me what I knew about them, I just sat there speechless because I could not say what I knew about the company.

I figured it would not be necessary to do research on a school district. It especially ate me inside because they said they were filling one teacher assistant position and one facility assistant position among me and four other interviewees. If you don't know the website to the company you will interview with, call the company to get their link before the day of your appointment. Memorize up to a handful of the most relevant bits of information.

Steps to take before an interview

The first important step to take is to have the right materials to present yourself in the most positive light possible when you go in to meet a recruiter or hiring manager. Instead of taking a backpack or ordinary book bag, take a briefcase or attaché – it may cost a few dozen bucks at a minimum but it should be worth it. Also, you should have enough appropriate outfits.

If you are a guy, have at least a few suits on hand. Your suit jackets and blazers should match your dress pants, dress shirt, dress shoes and dress socks. If you are a female, you should wear a good dress or a dress shirt along with dress pants and dress socks plus dress shoes. No matter what your gender is, make sure your dress shoes have a polished look.

Another vital step is to have a cover letter and resume that make a recruiter read them in their entirety instead of quickly discarding them; after all, they are busy souls and you only have seconds to grab their attention and compel them to keep reading. You will more extensively learn how to master these materials later in this book. In the meantime, we will discuss covering work history gaps on your resume.

If you get the reader to notice these gaps too much, he/she is likely to quickly drop you from consideration. You can make gaps in your work history less glaring by merely listing your skills at the front and middle of your resume and list the dates you worked at your former employers at the back. Also, it is in your best interests to conduct a Google search on a firm before applying or interviewing for the position to see if they have many poor reviews.

You never know when you may need to provide references. My general rule of thumb is to have the name, telephone number and maybe an email address available for three personal and three professional references, people you know will say something good about your character or performance. If you have done plenty of temp work, consider listing the people who have directly supervised your temp work at the sites where you have completed your assignments on good terms.

How to find and keep a job – section two

Offer vast flexibility as a temp. Because I neither indicated a willingness to work light industrial assignments (those that involve work such as lifting or moving light objects or cleaning out stores) when I registered with a staffing agency in 2000 nor accepted their offer to do a similar assignment a few years later, I had regrets as they cut ties with me and told me to stop calling them in 2005 due to my not working for them the past five years. Also, I upset the main recruiter for another temp agency due to not agreeing to an assignment at a call center located on a bus line because I was not enthusiastic about working at 7:00 AM even though the buses ran at that time in the early morning hours in 2006.

It's essential to make a dummy run, or advanced trip, to the place of your job interview, temp assignment or focus group study at least one day in advance because the location might take longer to reach and be harder to find than you think. Another option is to give yourself an extra 75 to 120 minutes to get there on the day you're scheduled to be there - it's especially crucial to give yourself this much time if you're a bus rider and thus could be on foot for a long time once you exit the bus. Adhere to either one of these recommendations no matter how well you've been given directions to the location.

You can make an exception to these suggestions when the place is on a major road and you are very familiar with the area. Because temp agencies are apt to assume that you have found a job elsewhere or are no longer interested in their services if they don't hear from you in a while, you must let yours know you are available for assignments weekly by telephone or email.

Finally, be more careful about taking a lunch break while doing temp work on a team. After I once had lunch while the rest of my team was not assigned to do so on a rotation basis in which the groups had the break one at a time in order to get the most production possible, a fellow temp warned me that if I did that again, the site supervisors could tell me that I was done doing the assignment.

Steps to take during the interview
Besides looking and smelling good, you must sit up straight, show willingness to work overtime, be willing to work at certain times on short notice, answer questions fully instead of being vague, have tact and be ready to answer lots of different questions. You can show tact by refraining from interrupting the hiring person, smiling genuinely, not having food or drinks in the open, not chewing gum, not using your cell phone, etc.

The questions you must prepare for include where you see yourself five years later, what they should learn about you, why they should choose you, what your biggest weakness is, etc. Good answers in this order are 1) you imagine becoming more valuable to the firm in five years, 2) you are qualified due to having the skills, training or experience, 3) you are the best one for the position and 4) you tend to be a perfectionist - keep in mind that you will have even more ease being poised and answering questions properly by relaxing and thinking of the person handling the hiring as your friend.

You must always be punctual in addition to maintaining a good attitude and hygiene - it is not smart to show up to an interview or go to work stinking from smoking/chewing tobacco or traveling a significant distance by foot or bicycle when it's hot outside. Bosses won't always tell you what you are doing wrong. During the summer of 1996, I continued always walking all the way to my college campus audiovisual assistant job even though it was too hot to do that, even in the mornings; consequently, I got smelly. Once while reaching over a co-worker who was training me to use the control room for the surrounding classrooms setting, he said, "Please don't reach your arm over me."

Next, he got up and didn't come back. He must have notified the boss of this because as my annual contract was coming to a close that August, the boss told me that not mastering the control room was partly why I was not being asked back and having my contract renewed. I fell a month short of remaining at a job I loved because I literally stank.

Also, do not show up to work or an appointment with your private area smelling bad - if you usually take a shower or bath every three days like I do, you must wash your private area over the bathroom sink within 24 to 33 hours after you last cleaned your entire body. When you brush your teeth upon getting out of bed, make sure to also brush your tongue, as bacteria that causes bad breath is on our tongues and between our teeth - using mouthwash is also a good idea.

You must also obey the rules and be open to learning on the job. Additionally, your immediate supervisor will surely not like it if you go over his/her head to report something at work - I almost lost the AV job discussed above for reporting a co-worker for copying movies to the campus police - little did I know you can do that as long as you don't reproduce and distribute the movies.

Having a positive attitude on the job is a must. Besides getting along with customers and the rest of the staff, you must take instruction well and not show anger. On my last day of working at a fast-food restaurant (my first job), the boss didn't like the way I was mopping the floor. After he told me that if I didn't start mopping faster, he didn't think he would keep me on the job after that day, I began mopping faster but frowned. I never saw my name on the schedule again there.

How to find and keep a job – section three

Never forgo checking up on your status after interviewing for a position, even if you are only lukewarm about it. Approximately ten years ago, the lady interviewing me for a hotel maintenance job told me she would love to have me in the housekeeping department. Even though I would have accepted the job if she had offered it to me, I did not follow up on it because I did not have as much desire to have it as I did before applying for it. That was a mistake because I have not had a steady job ever since.

Step to take after the interview
If you are not careful, you may end up getting underpaid or pricing yourself out of a job if you submit the first wage offer. Any counter offer you make should not be far above or below the company's offer.

How to find and keep a job – section four

In order to retain your job, you must always act professional, not silly like I once did. Because I once used a weird, high pitch while pointing toward the ceiling and excessively accentuating my voice to have more fun as a market research telephone interviewer, I had to see the division manager in her office.

You can get at least seven hours of sleep the night before going to work the next day and still fall asleep on the job, especially if you're making a lot of phone calls without getting many responses like I did while doing this interviewer job.

The first time I got caught napping, a supervisor called me from her station and said, "You better wake up."

Alarmed, I responded, "Okay."

The next time I was caught sleeping, this same supervisor took me into the office of the head supervisor on duty who thus told me that if I slept again, I would be sent home for the day and the incident would go into my files. You can avoid accidentally sleeping on the clock by standing up occasionally and when you get too drowsy.

Do not quit your position without finding another one first, no matter how good the job market is. Never walk away from a task, no matter how daunting it may seem.

After clocking out early from my in-store window display job due to slow foot traffic a second time in 1997, my boss chewed me out, "Don't do it anymore. I'm tired of it. If you can't be productive, I'm just going to fire you."

Speaking of the situation discussed above, keep in mind that you are a guest in the stores you work at through your company if you do in-store demos. You must dress decently, act professionally, treat everyone in the store including the staff with respect, avoid reading/studying in the open at your display booth, etc. Whether you're a regular employee or a guest worker at a store, do not leave tissue on the toilet seat and do not neglect to flush the toilet in the restroom.

One more suggestion for workers
Besides gauging the qualifications you have, employers want to see if you think fast on your feet, if you're motivated, etc. Exude energy, express your desire to be flexible, be ready to answer any question meant to throw you off at any time, etc.

How to write a cover letter

Your cover letter is your stepping stone to getting someone who reads resumes to look at yours – you can do this with a brief but well-written CV. What you must do on this document is give a little bit of your background that is pertinent to the position you are applying for, avoid using "I" too much and state why you are including your resume.

If you are responding to the position being advertised, point that out. If you have been referred by someone familiar with the recruiter, mention this. Following this up by making the rest of your letter and your resume great will help you get that important phone call.

All sentences that list your achievements, skills and duties in your CV and resume should begin will a bullet. To insert a bullet in Microsoft Word, choose Insert<Symbol then choose the bullet icon. Below are examples based on my most recent cover letter. Some of the information has been edited for clarity or privacy.

XXXXX@gmail.com
XXX-XXX-XXXX
March 10, 2016

Subject: Response to your ad for the Data Entry position that appeared on XYZ

Dear Sir or Madam:

My skills and experience are invaluable. My ambition is to go the extra mile while contributing to the success of your company. I think my skills will help me succeed.

Accomplishments and Background
- Strong computer and typing skills
- Improving the bottom line

My resume has been enclosed. Please contact me for an interview when you are ready. Thank you in advance for your consideration.

Sincerely,

Todd Hicks

How to write a resume

You just learned to limit using "I" statements in your cover letter; well, you must not use any of these in your resume. All of your statements and sentences must begin with an action verb. Proofread and edit your resume until there are no errors or typos - although the spell check feature in Word is pretty good for helping us catch our punctuation and grammar mistakes, it's not foolproof and thus requires us to add our own reviewing and attention to detail.

Besides using action verbs, you must jazz up your resume so that it makes you look like an achiever on the job rather than merely a doer - don't omit any job promotions or other big accomplishments you've had. Finally, your resume should cover the jobs you have had for the last seven to ten years at the most and not be longer than two pages.

If you don't have a lot of experience, especially the direct experience that pertains to jobs that may not necessarily be what you want, you can help cover this up by putting sections regarding your skills and other attributes at the front of your resume, with your actual job experience at the back like I have done.

Below is a model of my resume. I have edited this somewhat for clarity and privacy.

Todd Hicks 000-000-0000   XXXXXXXX@gmail.com

OBJECTIVE
- Seeking work that matches my passion and is a good fit for my background

CUSTOMER SERVICE AND DATA ENTRY EXPERIENCE
- Streamlined the membership process by professionally processing ABC Corporation's fund drive orders.
- Kept information up to date by updating the Membership database at ABC Corporation.
- Expedited office workflow by accurately filing papers and handling mailings at ABC Corporation.
- Assisted patrons with enthusiasm and delivered equipment to classrooms on time as a high school library aide.
- Delivered audiovisual equipment to classrooms on schedule through ABC Corporation.

LEADERSHIP AND MARKETING EXPERIENCE
- Conducted magnetic window display demonstrations that increased sales by hundreds of dollars for ABC Corporation.

- Promoted to window display trainer after producing more revenue through sales-producing leads.
- Taught new hires to do window display demos that increased ABC Corporation's leads and sales as a trainer at the management level.
- Quickly completed many of the clients' surveys at ABC Corporation.
- Produced leads that brought more sales to ABC Corporation.

SELF EMPLOYMENT EXPERIENCE
- Operate blogs that help people improve their lives.
- Write books that entertain and inform readers.
- Make voice heard by participating in consumer research.
- Help clients by doing their online tasks satisfactorily.
- Promote affiliate products and services.

LIST OF EMPLOYERS
Temp – October 2005 to Present
ABC Corporation

Substitute Teacher – August 2004 to May 2006
ABC School District

Substitute Teacher – September 2000 to June 2004
ABC School District

Membership Intern – January 2000 to May 2000
ABC Station

Telephone Interviewer/Market Researcher – July 1998 to April 2000
ABC Corporation

Window Display Person/Trainer – August 1996 to April 1998
ABC Corporation

Audiovisual Assistant – September 1995 to August 1996
ABC Corporation

Telemarketer – March 1995 to May 1995
ABC Corporation

COMPUTER AND TYPING SKILLS
• Word, Excel, Access, PowerPoint, Outlook, strong typing speed

EDUCATION
Bachelor of Arts in Communications, May 2000 – The University of Missouri at St. Louis

This wraps it up for formatting your cover letter and resume. In order to ensure that recruiters' computer systems can read your cover letter and resume, format these documents in a strong font like Times New Roman.

How to possibly keep your substitute teaching job

Being a substitute teacher can be fun but quite trying and hard to keep doing for a long time. Although I loved the students as a sub, I resented the way the school officials were unsupportive and figuratively stabbed me in the back.

As I had my first subbing job through one school district, the secretary who coordinated the process of calling in subs had no confidence in me and told my brother (a fellow sub for the district) that I wouldn't do what I was asked – when I called to ask her for elaboration, she said, "I just thought you looked too young. I might start calling you."

That never happened. I rarely got called in. At the end of that school year or the next one which was my last with that district, I did not get a letter inviting me to return for the upcoming school year. As I called to ask about that, the lady in the district administrative office who answered the telephone told me that because I had subbed less than five times for the year, I wasn't invited back and that they were getting strict on that. This situation occurred even though I made myself available to sub at all district schools Monday through Friday.

Unhappy that I wasn't called in to sub more, I explained that I didn't get the opportunity to sub more; however, the lady told me that if I could start subbing more, I should pay a reinstatement fee to reapply for the position. Having dignity, I refused to do that and subsequently became a sub at another area district. Here are three matters that got me in trouble with this district:

Failing to maintain a clean classroom
As the students had their coats on the floor one day, I thought nothing of it. The principal and a teacher who came in were unhappy with me.

Not maintaining class control
On another day, the students were noisy and unruly in my music class. Eventually, a

student asked if she could go get help. I wish I had not allowed her to go to the office because the principal was upset with me in addition to scolding the class. Although I have no regrets about it, I tried balancing compassion with maintaining an atmosphere conducive to learning - I liked issuing warnings and sending unruly students to the hall instead of the office. I wanted to avoid being a mean sub.

Being late
I was late a few times due to not gauging how much time I would have to arrive while accepting an invitation to sub on short notice. For example, if I got a call at 5:30 AM to show up at a school to work, I would accept the invitation not realizing that it would perhaps take as long as two hours to get ready to leave out then take the bus to the assigned location. I learned to not accept an invitation if I didn't think I would be able to arrive on time.

What to do as a sub
Once you get hired, take a trip to all schools in your district so that you know exactly where they are and how long it takes to get to them. By always being on time, maintaining order, keeping the classroom clean and being polite to everyone, you will give yourself a fighting chance of keeping your position. Last of all, you can ask the principals if they are satisfied with your work at the end of the school day.

In closing, I am pointing out that the situations discussed above led to the schools writing me up to the district personnel office behind my back. Besides being immoral, it was against district policy to not tell subs what they disliked about their performance according to what was said at the summer orientation meetings.

It's disgraceful that you can show up on time and do your best to follow the policies plus do your job well but still get written up without being told what you did wrong. This is what happened to me once again during my second year with the district; consequently, I was not allowed back. I then decided it wasn't worth it to apply to sub with more school districts.

How to present yourself in a speech, sales talk or job interview

In order to successfully talk in front of an audience, you must remain composed and establish a strong connection to build an ethos and credibility. In order to do personal sales or product demonstrations in stores, you must be professional and persuasive besides building a good rapport. To do well at an interview, you must sell yourself.

You will have more ease succeeding in every situation by carrying yourself well orally. By following the tips below, you will learn to persuade your audience, make a sales pitch that can lead to more conversions and make your case to a recruiter in person.

Public speaking tips
• Base your speech on a topic you are familiar and comfortable with.
• You can lighten the mood with a joke or small talk at the beginning.
• Only glance at your notes once in a while at best.
• Do not have your arms or legs crossed.
• Keep your hands out of your pockets.
• Frequently look at everyone, not just certain individuals.
• Perceive the audience as people being in your corner.
• Smile constantly.
• Avoid having an axe to grind, or ranting about something or someone you don't like.

Interpersonal sales tips
• Learn all you can about your product.

- Become more likable by smiling and being friendly toward everyone who comes your way.
- Move on and continue to be upbeat when people refuse to hear your pitch.
- If someone says he/she won't buy your product but hangs around, stay positive, quickly describe your item then politely send the patron away.
- If kids come by your station alone, acknowledge them and give them a quick demo - as a boy once came to my booth alone, I ignored him. As I greeted his mom as she came by, she said, "I'm not going to listen to what you have to say because you ignored my son."
- Have customers try out your item, if applicable.
- As you give your demo, listen to your prospects, answer their questions and explain how you can help solve their problems.

Interview presentation tips
- Break eye contact for a few seconds occasionally in order to make the recruiter comfortable.
- Do not answer questions in a vague or rambling manner.
- You should not ask about the salary or say something bad about your former or current bosses.
- Show up with a briefcase/attaché if you desire to bring items.

Please leave a review on your reading experience. The process is quick and easy: file:///C:/Users/Todd%20Hicks/AppData/Local/Temp/Temp1_Fiction.zip/Fiction/Fiction%20Reader%20Book%20Review%20Form.pdf

www.ingramcontent.com/pod-product-compliance
Lightning Source LLC
Chambersburg PA
CBHW050326220526
45465CB00005B/2150